D0450317

DIVINE EXCESS

DIVINE EXCESS

 Mexican Ultra-Baroque

Ichiro Ono

CHRONICLE BOOKS

SAN FRANCISCO

First published in the United States in 1996
by Chronicle Books.

Copyright © 1995 by Ichiro Ono.
All rights reserved. No part of this book
may be reproduced in any form without written
permission from the publisher.

First published in Japan in 1995
by Shinchosha Company, Ltd.

ISBN: 0-8118-1483-1

Printed in Hong Kong.

Library of Congress Cataloging-in-Publication
Data available.

Cover and text design: Livermore Design
Translation: Michiko Shigaki
and Thomas L. J. Daly

Distributed in Canada by
Raincoast Books
8680 Cambie Street
Vancouver, B.C. V6P 6M9

10 9 8 7 6 5 4 3 2 1

Chronicle Books
275 Fifth Street
San Francisco, California 94103

6   Cathedral, Zacatecas

Temple of San Augustine, Zacatecas

8~9   Church of San Sebastián and Santa Prisca, Taxco

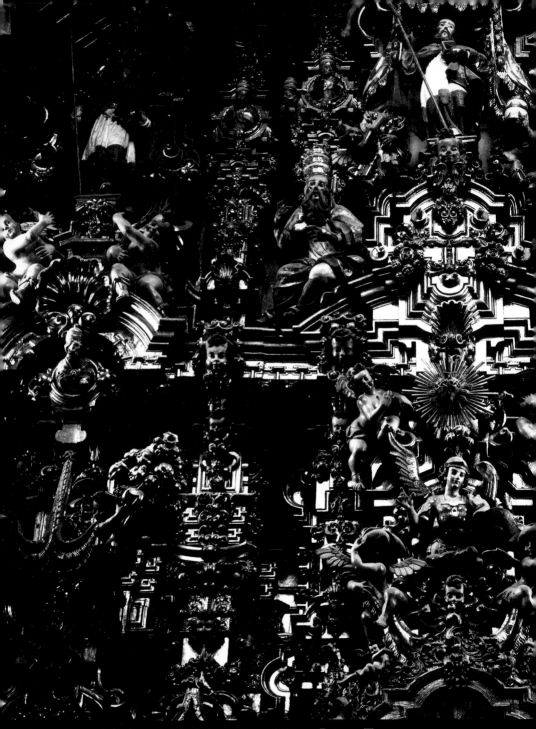

10~11   Church of San Sebastián and Santa Prisca, Taxco

12~13   Chapel of the Rosary, Puebla

14～15   Chapel of the Rosary, Puebla

16~17   Our Lady of Ocotlán Sanctuary, Tlaxcala

18~19　　Our Lady of Ocotlán Sanctuary, Tlaxcala

20~21   Niche, Our Lady of Ocotlán Sanctuary, Tlaxcala

22~23   Niche, Our Lady of Ocotlán Sanctuary, Tlaxcala

24~25   Church of Santo Domingo, Oaxaca

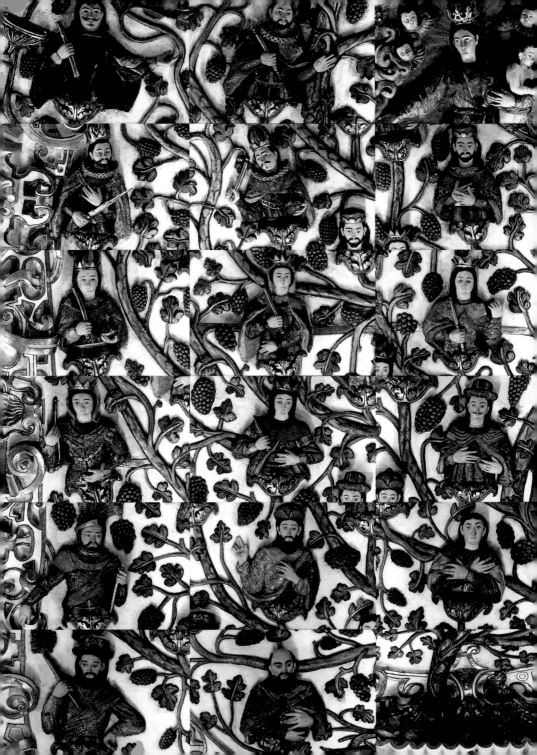

26~27   Church of Santo Domingo, Oaxaca

Church of the Prophet, Mexico City, D.F.

Church of San Sebastián and Santa Prisca, Taxco

Temple of Carmen, San Luis Potosi

Church of San Francisco, San Luis Potosi   35

Church of the Prophet, Mexico City, D.F.

Church of the Prophet, Mexico City, D.F.

Temple of Carmen, San Luis Potosi

Holy Week Procession, Puebla

Church of Santo Domingo, Tlacolula

Church of San Francisco Xavier, Tepotzotlan 45

46~47 Church of San Francisco Xavier, Tepotzotlan

56~57   Our Lady of Ocotlán Sanctuary, Tlaxcala

Church of San Diego, Guanajuato

Old Parish Church, Salamanca

Church of San Bernardino, Traxcalancingo

Church of San Francisco, Acatepec

JOSEP

SanctusDeus SanctusFortis SanctusIm mortal miserere

Church of San Lucas, Tzicatlan

Church of Santa Maria, Jolalpan

74~75   Cemetery, Night of the Day of the Dead

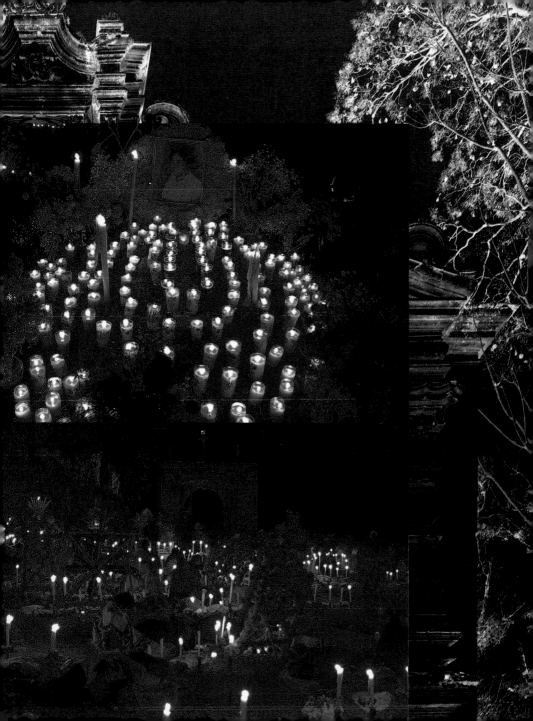

Offering, Day of the Dead, Janitzio

Temple of Santa Rosa, Antigua

Our Lady of the Sorrow of the Hill Hermitage, Antigua

Temple of Santa Rosa, Antigua   79

Temple of Carmen, Antigua

Temple of the Candelaria, Antigua   81

From Baroque to Ultra-Baroque

Ichiro Ono

What images does one conjure up when one hears the word "Mexico"? A man in a sombrero playing a guitar, lovely women in colorful dress, and traditional cuisine such as corn tamales? Or, residents of Mexico City suffering from air pollution, Chiapas farmers standing tall with firearms held high, or the crises in the currency? Or, for those with an artistic bent, it may be the pyramids of the Aztec and the Maya, the revolutionary frescos of Rivera and Siqueiros, Frida Kahlo, or Buñuel.

Whatever comes to mind, I think that pious, Catholic, baroque churches shining with gold may be unfamiliar as images of Mexico.

Art styles from all over the world poured in to Mexico in the colonial era of the sixteenth to early nineteenth centuries, reflecting the age of ocean trade. The term "baroque" originally referred to an irregular pearl, and the baroque style, imported from Europe during the mid-seventeenth century, was an extravagant departure from the sober, restrained styles of the Renaissance. Fused with ancient native American sensibility while absorbing other influences from the sea-trading world that collected in Mexico, the baroque style evolved and commenced to tightly pack the architecture with so much ornamentation that we could describe it as a kind of "gap-ophobia." This is "ultra-baroque," meaning, in other words, the baroque of the baroque.

It was in the 18th century that ultra-baroque reached its peak. During the mid-seventeenth century, due to restrictions placed on immigration from Spain, the power of new generations born in Mexico of Spanish lineage, called "criollos," and those of mixed European and Indian blood called "mestizos" began to rise. Consequently, Mexican architecture developed to reflect the tastes of those citizens who had attained economic power and had become patrons of the church; seeking after visible splendor became a primary interest. This set the groundwork to encourage the exploding popularity of the baroque style.

In the latter half of the seventeenth century, an architecture with the added originality of the indigenous culture appeared. Good examples are the Chapel of the Rosary in Puebla and the Church of Santo Domingo in Oaxaca. While the intermingling of bloodlines went on, some of the native Indian culture was absorbed into colonial society, and in ecclesiastical decoration the European baroque model came to take on a Mexican coloration, carrying vestiges of thousands of years of indigenous culture, including the sophisticated civilizations of the Mayas and Aztecs. These traditions may be glimpsed in a statue of a dark-complexioned Mary, or an Indian-looking angel peering out from a brilliantly colored jungle, or a saint whose head has been cut off as if he were a sacrificial offering, or a lively expression of suffering using the blood of animals.

Originally, the architectural styles introduced to Mexico after the conquest were regional Spanish types reflecting the seven-century history of Islamic domination in Spain, rather than pure Renaissance, Mannerist, or baroque. It seems to me that the oriental, Moorish taste imported with the Spanish inspired the creativity of the indigenous craftsmen in Mexico and contributed to the revival of the sensibilities of their ancestors.

The elaborately ornamented ultra-baroque churches in Mexico have an extremely simple architectural structure. While Europe's baroque style pursues dramatic spatial structure in three-dimensional depth, Mexican ultra-baroque pursues the supremacy of two-dimensional ornamentation to completely fill the overall surface. At that time in Europe, churches were built according to varied architectural plans, but in Mexico church plans are nearly identical if they fall within the same era. They applied a simple basic structure, which had a history of many successful examples, and the total effort concentrated on the visible areas while invisible areas were simplified.

~

"The Day of the Dead" in early November is the best time to observe that the ultra-baroque sensibility is alive among the people of Mexico even today. We can clearly see where Indian ceremonies to honor the dead are united with Western baroque festivity. Flowers and candies are everywhere, and all the streets and villages welcome the souls of the dead by competing with ornaments and colors.

We can see Mexican sensibilities in the statues of saints created by unknown craftsmen. Christ's rope-tied hands, his bruised legs, his face looking almost ecstatic. A beautiful Mary, sympathetic; and adorable infant, innocent angels. Their expressions are natural and even sensual. They have professional stylists who change their wigs and clothing, so the hair on the head of Christ switches between straight and curled. The religion here is not a silent praying in the deep bottom of one's mind, but is an intense experience directly stimulating to one's feelings. In the New World, these gaudy churches and lovely statues of Mary were aimed at impressing the absoluteness of Christianity upon the indigenous people and making newcomers contribute money for the greater glorification of God's home, to secure a place in heaven by enhancing their social positions on earth.

~

There is a theory that regions which embrace cultures that exhibit extravagant ornamentation are often riddled with earthquakes. Certainly the region from Mexico to Guatemala has suffered from major earthquakes. In Sicily, Catania, and Noto, which were rebuilt after being destroyed by eruptions from Mt. Etna, are magnificent baroque cities. Antigua in

Guatemala was a city as large as Mexico City or Lima and served as the capital of a governor-generalcy during the colonial era, but in the seventeenth century, recurrent great earthquakes brought it to ruin. Today, when we visit Antigua, ruins of the churches are scattered around, even in the woods outside of town, and we can muse on the prosperity of bygone days. I wonder what the baroque ornamentation remaining here and there in the ruined churches could tell us. The people must have known that the next earthquake would again reduce them to rubble. Even so, people ornamented the houses of God even more gorgeously when they were rebuilt. I wonder if it was because they sought God's help where destruction could visit at any time, and were driven by a desire to fill their world with beauty.

During the time I studied architecture in college, I spent a lot of time traveling seeking encounters with architecture. This was because I wanted to encounter an architecture that would energize my creativity. At first, I thought that such architecture would exist at the contact point of Eastern and Western cultures. So I trekked across only the Eurasian landmass, and it was a long time before I made a different journey to encounter the Mexican ultra-baroque. The extravagantly ornamented Mexican baroque would seem to be the absolute opposite of simple Japanese architecture. However, it seems to me that the essence hidden in the expression has something in common with some examples in Japanese temple architecture.

Even though I may be exploring the baroque, I do not want to take pictures of Western Europe's orthodox architectural styles. Like modern architecture, they do not stir my blood, nor am I interested in vernacular architecture. In short, modern universality and local folkloric traditions are not what appeal to me in themselves; my interest is in how to convey the aspects of ultra-baroque, established by the layers of struggle between the two, through my own consolidation. The traditional power of the indigenous people rages beyond the rules of western European architecture and the strictures of Catholicism even while attending to those rules. A thrill arises from the realization that destruction starts out from the details while at the same time the forces of integration continue on.

I, who am in the position to shoot, click the shutter at the contact point between the desire to make the whole thing simple and ordered and the desire to let it rage intricately and without limit. My desire to shoot something that truly attracts me means that I want to capture it as it is and bring it back without inserting my personal feelings, if possible. For me the act of shooting a photograph has the same import as the activity involved in collecting objects, such as by buying one's favorite chinaware or a gold-leafed statue of Mary. It might be better to say that I am a collector rather than a photographer.

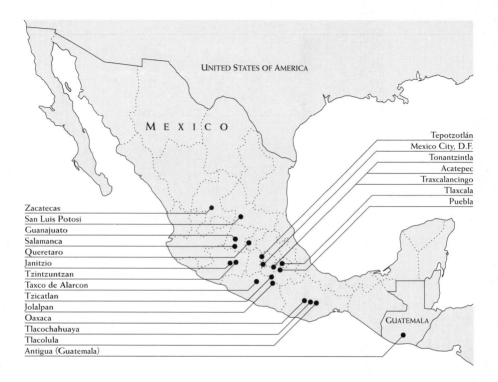

UNITED STATES OF AMERICA

M E X I C O

Tepotzotlán
Mexico City, D.F.
Tonantzintla
Acatepec
Traxcalancingo
Tlaxcala
Puebla

Zacatecas
San Luis Potosi
Guanajuato
Salamanca
Queretaro
Janitzio
Tzintzuntzan
Taxco de Alarcon
Tzicatlan
Jolalpan
Oaxaca
Tlacochahuaya
Tlacolula
Antigua (Guatemala)

GUATEMALA